P9-DVB-267

ESTRENO Collection of Contemporary Plays

General Editor: Martha T. Halsey

PASSAGE

FERMÍN CABAL

PASSAGE

Translated by Rick Hite

ESTRENO
University Park, Pennsylvania
1998

ESTRENO Contemporary Spanish Plays
General Editor: Martha T. Halsey
                       Department of Spanish, Italian and Portuguese
                       College of the Liberal Arts
                       The Pennsylvania State University
                       University Park PA 16802 USA

Cataloging Data
Cabal, Fermín, 1948-
     Passage
     Translation of: Travesía
     Contents: Passage
     1. Cabal, Fermín, 1948- Translation, English
I. Hite, H. Rick II. Title.
Library of Congress Catalog Card No.: 97-60261
     ISBN: 1-888463-03-1

© 1998 Copyright by ESTRENO

Original play © Fermín Cabal: Travesía, 1993.

Translation © H. Rick Hite 1998

The publishers wish to acknowledge with thanks
financial assistance for this translation from the
Dirección General del Libro y Bibliotecas
of the Ministerio de Cultura de España.

Cover: Jeffry Eads

A NOTE ON THE PLAY

Let's face it, the reason most of us live our lives as comedy instead of as tragedy is that our flaws are forming rather than transforming us. Fermín Cabal's *Passage*, in that sense and in others, is definitely a comedy. But what kind?

There are lots of familiar ingredients here: a lovers' triangle set in the hermetic yet libidinous atmosphere of a tropical cruise. (An unhappy couple, Domingo and Mariana, are taking passage to an exotic otherness they hope will be elemental enough to break them loose from the deceits and betrayals they have refined into unintentional self-mockery. Lucas, the loner and old Africa-hand, has the [mis]fortune to be in the stateroom next to theirs.) Much of the play is an intricate *ronde* of incriminating entrances and exits--through doors and in and out of beds. Is it farce?

Cabal gives one prop--a pistol--so much personality that it almost seems to be a fourth cast member. It is flamboyantly ineffectual like the one Uncle Vanya fires at the end of the third act of his namesake play. Is this Chekhovian comedy?

The characters are recognizable contemporaries, but the Spanish context is also felt. Two brilliantly balletic duels at the ping-pong table are vintage Cabal: his sly way of puncturing what is left of machismo. So... is it post-modern slap-stick? Or satire, pure and simple?

I choose none of these, feeling that Fermín Cabal has reached the point where he deserves recognition for creating a uniquely original comic genre all his own. My candidate for the title is... dangerous comedy.

Rick Seyford
Department of Theater
Mary Baldwin College

FERMÍN CABAL

ABOUT THE PLAYWRIGHT

Fermín Cabal, born in León in 1948, is one of the generation of Spanish theater artists who formed the independent theater movement. In his early career he worked as actor, director, and playwright with such groups as Tábano, Los Goliardos, and El Gayo Vallecano. By the end of the seventies and into the eighties he became recognized as one of Spain's important new voices in the theater with his plays, *Tú estás loco, Briones* (*You're Crazy, Briones*) (1978), *¿Fuiste a ver a la abuela?* (*Did You Go to See Grandmother?*) (1979), *¡Vade retro!* (*Get Thee Behind Me!*) (1982), and *Esta noche, gran velada* (*Big Bash Tonight*) (1983). In 1985 Cabal co-authored with J. L. Alonso de Santos *Teatro español de los 80*, a collection of interviews with the leading theater artists of their generation. His next play, *Caballito del diablo* (*Dragonfly*), came out the same year, and in 1986 he wrote his first filmscript, *La reina del mate* (*Checkmate Queen*). From 1986 to 1988 he wrote the television series, *Ramper*. Then in 1990 he returned to the stage with his play, *Ello dispara* (*It Shoots*). This was followed by *Entre tinieblas* (*Dark Habits*) (1992), a play based on Pedro Almodóvar's film of the same name, *Travesía* (*Passage*) (1993, winner of the Tirso de Molina prize in 1991), and *Castillos en el aire* (*Castles in the Air*) (1995). Cabal has also translated and adapted several American plays for the Spanish stage, including David Mamet's *American Buffalo* and Christopher Durang's *Beyond Therapy*. His most recent writing has been for the Spanish version of the American sitcom, *The Golden Girls*, for Television of Spain.

Travesía. Príncipe Gran Vía Theater, Madrid, 1993. Directed by Fermín Cabal.
Luisa Martínez (Mariana), Santiago Ramos (Domingo), Emilio Gutiérrez Caba (Lucas). Photo: Chicho.

CHARACTERS

MARIANA
LUCAS
DOMINGO

Onboard a ship. Upstage is a cabin. Two doors connect the cabin with a bath and the deck. The railing of the ship's deck is downstage. Between the two areas there is sufficient space to locate whatever elements the action demands: ping-pong table, deck chairs, etc.

An immense sky-cyclorama surrounds the stage.

MARIANA leans on the railing looking silently out to sea. The cyclorama subtly changes color.

MARIANA crosses towards the cabin and enters it. She picks up a book from the bed. She looks at it curiously. She sits on the bed and leafs through it. She lies back on the bed and reads the book.

Pause.

MARIANA appears to smell something strange. She takes the bedspread and sniffs it. She sits up. She sees a pair of pants on the floor. She gets up and folds the pants. A bunch of coins fall out of the pocket. She starts to pick them up.

The bathroom door opens and LUCAS appears, his face lathered, half shaved. He looks at her.

MARIANA (*On her knees*): Oh, excusez moi. Je m'ai trompé...
LUCAS: Je me suis trompé.
MARIANA: Vous etés? Ça c'est pas votre camarote?
LUCAS: Oui, ça c'est mon camarote, bien sure. Vous êtes doublement trompé.
MARIANA (*Indicating the coins she has in her hand*): Moi, je suis confusé.
LUCAS: Ça va pas la peine. Vous êtes espagnole, n'est pas?
MARIANA: Oh, oui. Vous l'avez connu pour l'accent?
LUCAS: Pas de tout. I heard you two talking last night. I'm Spanish too. Is your husband feeling better?
MARIANA: Oh..., yes, I think so. I didn't realize the walls were so thin. Did we make a lot of noise?
LUCAS: No, don't worry. It caught my attention hearing Spanish voices, and I just stood by the door for a moment, listening... But please, get up. I'll get those later.

(*MARIANA gets up.*)

MARIANA: You're probably wondering what I'm doing here.

LUCAS: No, really. You needed change?

MARIANA: I got the wrong cabin. It's unbelievable, exactly like ours... The bed, the night stand... even the painting.

LUCAS: Just as bad.

MARIANA: Yes. There must be a whole series.

LUCAS: Sold by the yard. It wouldn't surprise me.

(*Pause.*)

MARIANA: You said you were listening behind the door?

LUCAS: Involuntarily. I was about to come in. Forgive me, please.

MARIANA: No. What for? What else could you do?

LUCAS: Is your husband still angry?

(*Pause.*)

MARIANA: How much did you hear?

LUCAS: Well... I got curious. I thought, great, my neighbors are Spanish. I've done this trip a few times, and this is the first time I've run into other Spaniards. Passengers here are usually French, and Belgians, mostly. Keep to themselves, you know. Nothing wrong with them. Just keep to themselves. (*MARIANA watches him without saying anything.*) But don't worry, when the thing started getting personal, I stopped listening.

MARIANA: Nice of you.

LUCAS: You don't believe me?

MARIANA: Why should I believe you? I don't know you from Adam.

LUCAS: I don't know you either, but I still believe you. I come into my cabin and find you rifling my pants, with the money in your hand. I could think the worst, and with better reason.

MARIANA: I swear to you I got the wrong cabin.

LUCAS: And I believe you. And I apologize for my indiscretion. Word of honor, as soon as I realized, I stopped listening. In fact, I put on music.

MARIANA: The Walküre.

LUCAS: Exactly.

MARIANA: Very appropriate.

(*Pause.*)

MARIANA: My husband, when he's not feeling well, gets into an unbearable humor, and yesterday he was feeling a little seasick. The water was a little rough.

LUCAS: Well, that was nothing. When the ocean here gets really rough, it'll clean out your whole system.

MARIANA: Oh... really?

LUCAS: The Portuguese, who were the first Europeans to navigate these waters, believed the world ended out here. Imagine, with those little boats, what that had to be like? They noticed that the farther south they went the hotter it got, so they believed they'd reach a point where the water would start boiling. If it hadn't been for that, they'd have reached India a lot sooner. They dreamed up all kinds of legends, fabulous creatures, mermaids, monsters...

MARIANA: Are you a sailor?

LUCAS: No. I read about it in a book.

MARIANA: *The Conquest of the Atlantic*?

LUCAS: Right. You know it? Oh, of course.

(He notices that the book is on the nightstand.)

MARIANA: I was just leafing through it. It caught my eye.

LUCAS: Take it if you want. I've finished it.

(LUCAS picks up the book.)

MARIANA: No, don't bother.

LUCAS: And tell your husband if he gets seasick again, I have some pills that work very well.

(LUCAS gives her the book.)

MARIANA: Thanks. Good. Well... my pleasure.

(MARIANA offers LUCAS her hand. LUCAS wipes his off with his towel before shaking hers.)

LUCAS: Likewise. My name's Lucas.

MARIANA: Mariana Alzola.

LUCAS: You're Basque, right?

MARIANA: Right. I'm Basque.

LUCAS: Great navigators. You'll love the chapter on whaling.
MARIANA: I'll be sure to read it. Well, I suppose we'll see each other...
LUCAS: For sure. Can't avoid it here.
MARIANA: We'll try not to make so much noise. Goodbye.
LUCAS: Goodbye.

(*MARIANA leaves. LUCAS picks up his pants and goes into the bathroom.*)

(*MARIANA comes into the cabin and puts the book on the nightstand.*)

MARIANA: Domingo!

(*DOMINGO answers from the bathroom.*)

DOMINGO (*Off*): What?
MARIANA: I did a really dumb thing.
DOMINGO: You what?
MARIANA: I did a really dumb thing.

(*DOMINGO comes out of the bathroom.*)

DOMINGO: What did you do now?
MARIANA: I walked into some man's cabin.
DOMINGO: You what?
MARIANA: By mistake. (*Laughs.*) He was shaving.
DOMINGO: So no big deal.
MARIANA: It's just that when I went to fold his pants, all the money fell out on the floor... and I got down to pick it up, and that's when he caught me.
DOMINGO: Oh, that's great! What you are... is an idiot! So what did he do?
MARIANA: Nothing. He was very nice. We started speaking French.
DOMINGO: Well, of course, you're so good at that.
MARIANA: He told me things about the Portuguese. About the first voyages to Africa...
DOMINGO: Before or after taking off his pants?
MARIANA: Don't start... I'm telling you...
DOMINGO: What are you telling me?
MARIANA: I'm telling you I went into the next cabin by mistake, and I met...
DOMINGO: Some phoney Frenchy who starts telling you stories while you're folding his pants for him...

MARIANA: Domingo!

DOMINGO: Well, what do you want me to think?

MARIANA: But it wasn't like that...

DOMINGO: Look, you've got me... you've got me all...

MARIANA: The pants were on the bed when I went in. No, I mean, on the floor. I went to lie down on the bed and then...

DOMINGO: So, you were lying on the bed?

MARIANA: Just for a second! I saw the pants on the floor, and I started to pick them up...

DOMINGO: To get back at me.

MARIANA: Get back at you?

DOMINGO: To get back at me, same as always...

MARIANA: I thought they were yours...

DOMINGO: Fuck this shit. The minute we get to Malabo I put you on a plane and you go home.

MARIANA: You're still angry.

DOMINGO: What?

MARIANA: You're still angry. You said we'd call a truce, but you're still angry.

DOMINGO: Mariana. I've had it up to here. For twenty-four hours I've been throwing up, thanks to you...

MARIANA: Thanks to me.

DOMINGO: Whose idea was it to take this damned boat?

MARIANA: I thought it would be good for you, your stress...

DOMINGO: My stress? You thought seven days stuck in this cabin would be good for my stress?

MARIANA: People take cruises to relax.

DOMINGO: But this is not a cruise. This is the merchant marine!

MARIANA: What difference does it make? What matters is we have a few days to ourselves... to talk... to be together... to get back together... We said we'd start over again. In Africa.

DOMINGO: And the first thing you do is slip into the guy-next-door's cabin.

MARIANA: By mistake.

DOMINGO: Exactly. The whole thing is a mistake.

(*Pause.*)

DOMINGO: Have you seen my glasses?

MARIANA: No

(*Pause.*)

DOMINGO: My head's about to split.
MARIANA: You still feel sick?
DOMINGO: How do you expect me to feel? You and your damned ideas.
MARIANA: He offered me some pills for seasickness.
DOMINGO: The Frenchy?
MARIANA: He offered me some, for you.
DOMINGO: And why did you have to tell him about it?
MARIANA: He heard you last night. The walls are like paper. He ask me if you were feeling better.
DOMINGO: Who is this turkey? He'll try to take us for a ride!
MARIANA: Shhh! He'll hear us.
DOMINGO: And I'm supposed to worry? Fuck France! Brigitte Bardot is a piece of shit! And Camembert smells like farts! Pedants! The whole bunch! Althusser got it off by chopping up his wife! And Simone de Beauvoir, the whore, liked to do it with the girls in her class!
MARIANA: You're pathetic.
DOMINGO (*Calming down*): The French make me puke. (*Pause.*) They're like you. Everything has to be just what they say and the way they say it. (*Pause.*) You know they're trying to get the government of Guinea to make French the official language?
MARIANA: He's Spanish.
DOMINGO: Who? (*Pause.*) Our friend next door is Spanish? Which means he'll try to take us for a ride.
MARIANA: So far he's only offered us some pills.
DOMINGO: Tell him to take 'em and shove 'em.
MARIANA: I should go and tell him that?
DOMINGO: There's the door.
MARIANA: OK. We'll see, Mr. Know-it-all.

(*MARIANA exits, considerably riled.*)

DOMINGO: Mariana!... (*Angry.*) Damned bitch!

(*DOMINGO sits down on the bed. He belches. He is not feeling well.*)

(*MARIANA comes in followed by LUCAS.*)

MARIANA: Come in. My husband, Domingo... Lucas, from next door.

(DOMINGO glares at her. He falls back on the bed.)

MARIANA: Do you want to throw up?

DOMINGO: No, it's nothing.

LUCAS: I brought you some pills.

DOMINGO: I appreciate it. Thanks, really. I'm feeling better now.

MARIANA: You just finished saying you were seasick.

DOMINGO: Anyway, I stopped vomiting.

MARIANA: Right. Because you haven't eaten anything.

LUCAS: The pills will do the trick. A glass of water, please.

DOMINGO: Look I don't want pills.

MARIANA: Why?

DOMINGO: I don't like taking medicine.

LUCAS: I work in a mission hospital, if that makes you feel any better.

MARIANA: You're a doctor?

LUCAS: Nurse. Kind of improvised really. In Mopti you end up doing a little
   bit of everything.

DOMINGO: Missionary, huh?... So, now it's the Church we're butting heads
   with!

LUCAS: Of course, if you don't want to take them, don't take them. I assure
   you they're not dangerous. Read the label.

DOMINGO: That's another thing. Where are my glasses?

LUCAS: Are they over here?.

DOMINGO: Where did you put them?

MARIANA: I told you I don't know.

(MARIANA looks for the glasses.)

DOMINGO: I'm trying to read the label, and I can't find my damned glasses.

MARIANA: When did you last see them?

DOMINGO: When do you think? When I had them on. And when you took
   them off, I stopped seeing them. The glasses and everything else. I
   started throwing up. Don't you remember?

MARIANA: Yes,... You were reading when you got sick. That's right.

DOMINGO: And you took them off, and you started throwing water on me.

MARIANA: They must be in the bathroom...

(MARIANA exits into the bathroom. Pause.)

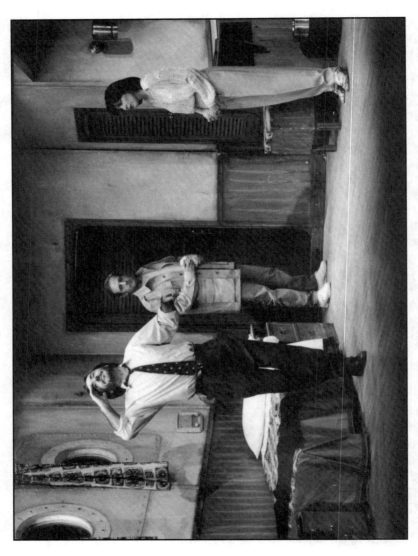

Travesía. Príncipe Gran Vía Theater, Madrid, 1993. Directed by Fermín Cabal. Santiago Ramos, Emilio Gutiérrez Caba, Luisa Martínez. Photo: Chicho.

DOMINGO: It's like this all day. She takes things, and then she doesn't know where she put them.

LUCAS: If you were seasick, you shouldn't have been reading.

DOMINGO: Listen, look, I appreciate your well intentioned interest, but I'm a big boy, you know?, and I really don't like people telling me what to do. So, in my cabin, I do whatever I damn well want to do, pardon the frankness. So, if I say I don't want pills, I mean I don't want pills. Period.

(MARIANA comes back from the bathroom.)

MARIANA: They're not in the bathroom.

DOMINGO: Of course they're not. You took them off out here, and then you took me to the bathroom.

LUCAS: Well, excuse me, I'll leave you then. If you change your mind, I'm right next door. First door on the right.

DOMINGO: I'll give a yell. I know you've got good ears.

MARIANA: You don't have to be rude.

LUCAS: No, really...

MARIANA: He came over to help.

DOMINGO: It's a joke, woman... Sorry. My nerves... The damned glasses... seasick stomach... I think it's coming on again...

LUCAS: You look a little pale.

DOMINGO: I do?

MARIANA: And sweaty.

(DOMINGO sits down on the bed. They start fanning him.)

DOMINGO: Those pills... What've they got in them?

LUCAS: Pyridoxine.

DOMINGO: Well that certainly clears that up. Won't it have side effects?

LUCAS: Read the label.

DOMINGO: Without my glasses.

LUCAS: I'll read it for you.

(LUCAS takes the box of pills.)

DOMINGO: Listen, what about a little whisky, wouldn't that help?

LUCAS *(Reading)*: Pills are contraindicated for alcohol.

DOMINGO: But I haven't taken them yet.

LUCAS: Same thing if you take them after.
MARIANA: Don't be so pig-headed. You're like a little child.
DOMINGO: I'm just seasick. It's OK. Get me a glass of water.

(*MARIANA goes into the bathroom.*)

DOMINGO: Oh, God, here we go again...
LUCAS: Sit down. Let's get a little air.

(*LUCAS helps him sit down.*)

DOMINGO: Aaaggghhh!
LUCAS: Are you going to vomit?
DOMINGO: I'm going to shit a brick!
LUCAS: What?
DOMINGO: I just sat on my glasses!

(*DOMINGO shows him the broken glasses. He starts to retch and runs off into the bathroom.*)

(*LUCAS crosses down to the railing. He looks out at the sea in silence. The light on the cyclorama changes. Night.*)

(*MARIANA comes out of the cabin and crosses to LUCAS.*)

LUCAS: Is your husband feeling better?
MARIANA: He's fallen asleep. (*Pause.*) So silent. Isn't it? (*Pause.*) The ocean has such a neutral sound. (*Pause.*) I mean, it's like a *sonorous* silence.
LUCAS: Have you ever been in the desert?
MARIANA: No. Never.
LUCAS: There's an impressive silence. No sound at all. (*Pause.*) A person coughs and you can hear it for twenty miles.
MARIANA: Twenty miles?
LUCAS: Well, I don't know exactly. A long way. (*Pause.*) One time we heard a man who was walking our way. We could hear his steps, but we couldn't see him. He appeared an hour later.
MARIANA: An hour?
LUCAS: An hour, more or less.

(*Pause.*)

MARIANA: Then that wouldn't have been more than six miles.
LUCAS: From the time we first saw him he was another hour getting to where we were camped.

(*Pause.*)

MARIANA: What was he doing walking out on the desert?
LUCAS: He was going home. (*Pause.*) He must have seen the smoke and come out of his way. He got there, greeted us, sat down quite nonchalantly, and had some tea.
MARIANA: And?...
LUCAS: And then he left. I tried inviting him to eat, but he said his family was waiting dinner, and it wasn't right for him to eat and them not. I tried to give him food for all of them, but he was offended. Apparently he came by in case we needed help. They're very proud, the Tuareg.
MARIANA: Incredible.
LUCAS: Finally I got him to take some provisions in exchange for this necklace.

(*From inside his shirt LUCAS pulls a leather thong with a sea shell covered with inlay work.*)

MARIANA: It's a shell.
LUCAS: They use these for money. It looks like it's worth something.
MARIANA: To them?
LUCAS: To me too. I believe that man taught me a lesson. Things can't just be given away, gratis.
MARIANA: Why not?
LUCAS: Because then they're not worth anything.

(*Pause.*)

MARIANA: But sometimes, I don't know, you run into someone in trouble, that same Tuareg, with a broken leg, in the middle of the desert. Wouldn't he accept your help?
LUCAS: Of course. He wouldn't have any choice. But he would pay a very high price. The highest. He'd end up obligated to me forever. Until he could give back to me what I gave him.

MARIANA: That seems terrible.

LUCAS: Why?

MARIANA: I don't know, it just seems terrible. Things are simpler than that.

LUCAS: Maybe.

(*Pause.*)

MARIANA: Would you react the same way?

LUCAS: I don't know. I'm a sinner.

(*Pause.*)

MARIANA: So... you live in the desert?

LUCAS: No. Our mission is in the Niger River basin. Bambara territory. But the desert is not far. You can smell it. In fact, everyday it gets a few feet closer.

MARIANA: Yes, I read something in the papers. They've had years of drought, right?

LUCAS: A disaster. Cutting the Amazon rain-forest has influenced the whole weather pattern. That's where the summer cloud masses form. And the winds drag them across the Atlantic for the rainfall in West Africa. Cutting trees in one place means less water in another.

MARIANA: The paper companies are to blame. If people knew how many trees you have to cut to get out the evening edition...

LUCAS: You think they'd stop reading it?

MARIANA: Little by little there's a growing consciousness about destroying the planet. Even if it's all just pure egoism...

LUCAS: Pure egoism that plants trees at home and cuts down its neighbor's. That's what's happening in the United States.

MARIANA: God, what a mess.

LUCAS: Yea.

(*Pause.*)

MARIANA: Are you a communist?

LUCAS: Me? You're saying that because of my dig about the Americans? No. No, I'm nothing.

MARIANA: No, of course. These days communism is passé. (*Pause.*) I was a communist. Well, a sympathizer. When I was at the university. I suppose I didn't keep myself very well informed about much... No, no that's not true. I kept myself pretty well informed, and it seemed a very good thing. We would spend hours reading Marx and Lenin. Book after book. Tons of trees consumed for the Manifesto, the Anti-Düring, the critique of the Gotha program, Das Kapital... whole forests... The first gift my husband gave me when we started going together was *The Sayings of Chairman Mao*. I mean, I was a bit of a Maoist. I used to go to parties and talk about how we all ought to become guerrillas. (*Pause.*) A lot of priests would agree. You never...?

LUCAS: No, never... The tropics are uncomfortable enough just by themselves without having to complicate it more. (*Pause.*) Besides, I think the revolutionary process is socially retarding.

MARIANA: What's that supposed to mean?

LUCAS: It means they're not worth what they cost. I told you, I don't believe in politics.

MARIANA: What do you believe in then? Wait, I know. You're going to say God.

LUCAS: I'm not really sure I believe in God.

MARIANA: No?

LUCAS: Let's say I believe in love. (*Pause.*) It's supposed to be the basis of western Christian civilization. Love thy neighbor as thyself. At least theoretically.

MARIANA: Too much theoretically, I'm afraid.

LUCAS: You're right on that one.

(*Pause.*)

(*LUCAS crosses toward the cabin. MARIANA exits.*)

(*He turns on the table lamp. He picks up a book, and flops down on the bed. He reads.*)

(*MARIANA comes out of the bathroom wearing a silk dressing gown. LUCAS stops reading. He looks at her. MARIANA lets the gown slip off her shoulders. She's naked under it. LUCAS closes the book.*)

(*DOMINGO, downstage, leaning on the ship's rail, looks out to sea. Change of light on the cyclorama. Day.*)

(*DOMINGO observes the ping-pong table on deck. LUCAS comes out of the cabin.*)

LUCAS: Good morning.
DOMINGO: Hello! Great morning!
LUCAS: Yes...
DOMINGO: I think the worst is over. You play ping-pong?
LUCAS: You look completely recovered.
DOMINGO: I slept well. So, a game?

> (*LUCAS goes to the table. He picks up a paddle. DOMINGO takes off his jacket. He picks up the other paddle.*)

DOMINGO: Been years since I played this. What do you think?
LUCAS: I'm really bad, but I'll give it a try.
DOMINGO: Shall we hit some?

> (*DOMINGO puts the imaginary ball in play. On the fifth hit he slams a point.*)

LUCAS: That wasn't bad...
DOMINGO: Guess once you have it you don't lose it. (*LUCAS serves one. DOMINGO returns, and LUCAS slams a point.*) Good! (*DOMINGO goes after the ball, but it bounces back towards LUCAS.*) There it is, get it...

> (*LUCAS retrieves the ball.*)

LUCAS: Volley for serve?
DOMINGO: Whatever. Shall we play a game?
LUCAS: How many points?
DOMINGO: Eleven?
LUCAS: Let's see who serves.

> (*LUCAS serves. On the fifth hit the ball goes out. DOMINGO gets it. DOMINGO serves. LUCAS returns high. DOMINGO catches it. DOMINGO serves. LUCAS nets the return. LUCAS picks up the ball and throws it to DOMINGO. DOMINGO serves.*)

DOMINGO: Last night (*hits the ball and LUCAS returns*) you two (*hits and LUCAS returns*) were up talking till very late?

> (*DOMINGO hits and LUCAS misses the ball. He goes for it.*)

LUCAS: Sorry?

DOMINGO: ...if you were up very late talking last night. My wife and you.

LUCAS: Well... we talked for a while, yes... Tell you the truth, I don't know what time it was...

(LUCAS throws the ball. DOMINGO catches it in the air.)

DOMINGO: Right. Lost track of the time, huh? *(DOMINGO serves. On the fifth hit he takes the point. LUCAS goes chasing the ball.)* My wife is a great conversationalist. *(LUCAS throws him the ball.)* Doesn't do much else. But talk... *(DOMINGO serves. LUCAS fails to return and chases the ball.)* Whitewash! *(LUCAS hands him the ball. DOMINGO hands it back.)* No. You serve. Five, zero. Every five points...

LUCAS: Yea. Right. *(LUCAS serves and misses.)* Fault.

DOMINGO *(Handing him the ball)*: This morning nothing could get her out of bed.

(LUCAS serves again and misses.)

LUCAS: Double fault.

DOMINGO *(Giving him the ball)*: Six, zero.

LUCAS: People sleep a lot at sea. *(Serves.)*

DOMINGO: Really? *(Returns.)*

LUCAS: What they say. *(Returns.)*

DOMINGO: Why? *(Returns.)*

LUCAS: I don't know. *(Wins the point.)*

DOMINGO: Good shot! Yes, sir. *(Goes for the ball.)* Six, one. *(Tosses him the ball.)* Closing the gap. *(LUCAS serves an ace.)* Now he's cooking. *(DOMINGO tosses LUCAS the ball. LUCAS serves. On the eighth hit DOMINGO sends it out.)* Six, three. *(LUCAS chases after the ball.)* Shit... *(LUCAS serves. DOMINGO smashes it back, and LUCAS nets his return.)* Seven, three. Change serve.

(LUCAS gets the ball and tosses it to DOMINGO.)

(MARIANA comes out to the deck area. She is wearing a bathing suit with a towel around it. She carries a deckchair. She waves to the players.)

DOMINGO: And there she is. *(Serves.)*

LUCAS: Huh?

(LUCAS looks back and almost misses the ball but snags it. DOMINGO doesn't expect the return and swings late.)

(MARIANA lies back on the deckchair. She starts reading the book LUCAS has lent her.)

DOMINGO: Damn. He's getting lucky. *(Going after the ball.)* Seven, four. Ready? *(DOMINGO serves. LUCAS nets the return. He gets the ball. DOMINGO serves again. On the sixth hit LUCAS sends it out. DOMINGO chases it down.)* Nine, four. Are you headed for Guinea too? *(Serves.)*
LUCAS: I'm staying in Akra. *(Returns.)*
DOMINGO: Business? *(Returns.)*
LUCAS: Kind of. *(Wins the point. DOMINGO goes after the ball.)* I'm bringing a Land-Rover from Spain. Used.
DOMINGO: Used?
LUCAS: That's all the budget can handle.
DOMINGO: And that's legal? *(Serves.)*
LUCAS: What? *(Returns.)*

(DOMINGO wins the point. LUCAS chases the ball. Waves to MARIANA.)

DOMINGO: Anyone who wants to can just bring a car in like that? *(LUCAS gestures at throwing him the ball.)* Ten, five. You serve. Match point.

(LUCAS serves. Smashing return by DOMINGO. LUCAS goes chasing the ball.)

LUCAS: You look in pretty good form to me. Maybe you're doped up on those pills?
DOMINGO: Another?
LUCAS: Enough for today.

(They put the paddles on the table.)

DOMINGO:I ask you about that because it's exactly what I'm looking into: the whole matter of importation of equipment. It's a complicated business.
LUCAS: Right now the car's coming in under my name as a tourist. Then we'll see.

DOMINGO: I see.
LUCAS: We really need it for the work at the mission.
DOMINGO: No, really, I understand perfectly.

(*They go over to where MARIANA is.*)

DOMINGO: Hello, love.
LUCAS: Good morning.
MARIANA: Good morning.
DOMINGO: How did you sleep?
MARIANA: Fine. Only,... Are there spiders on a boat?
DOMINGO: Spiders? I don't think so.

(*MARIANA lifts her towel and points to her thigh.*)

MARIANA: This looks like a spider bite, doesn't it?
LUCAS: Could be.
MARIANA: It's not a mosquito bite.
LUCAS: No. Doesn't look like it.
DOMINGO: You think they'll have to amputate?
LUCAS: That won't be necessary. I've got some cream for bites.
MARIANA: No, don't bother.
LUCAS: It's no bother.

(*LUCAS goes into the cabin.*)

(*DOMINGO sits on a deck chair next to MARIANA.*)

DOMINGO: You thinking about competing for Miss Africa? (*Pause.*) With
    that exhibition of legs...
MARIANA: What a twisted mind.
DOMINGO: My wife yanks up her skirt in front of some guy she doesn't
    know, and I'm supposed to stand there and take it.
MARIANA: I didn't yank up my skirt.
DOMINGO: You didn't?
MARIANA: I lifted the towel. And underneath it I'm wearing a bathing suit.
DOMINGO: I don't see the difference.
MARIANA: A skirt is the same thing as a towel?
DOMINGO: What difference is there?
MARIANA: The same as between a towel and a pair of pants.

DOMINGO: Maybe it wasn't a spider that bit you last night...?
MARIANA: When?
DOMINGO: When you were with him.
MARIANA: With him?
DOMINGO: Yes. Weren't you in his cabin?
MARIANA: But, what are you saying?
DOMINGO: You know very well.
MARIANA: Last night I wasn't in his cabin.
DOMINGO: You weren't in his cabin.
MARIANA: No!
DOMINGO: Where were you then? In the bar? In a lifeboat? In the crow's nest looking at the stars? Since you're such a romantic...
MARIANA: Don't start with your paranoia.
DOMINGO: You two were probably reciting the rosary together.
MARIANA: We were simply talking like two normal people.
DOMINGO: You're looking for a slap in the face...
MARIANA: You're crazy...

(MARIANA gets up and walks away from him. She exits. DOMINGO exits behind her.)

DOMINGO: You can't take a joke!

(LUCAS comes out of the cabin with the tube of cream. He discovers that the two have disappeared. He returns to the cabin.)

(MARIANA comes out of the bathroom and lies down on the bed. LUCAS comes into the cabin.)

LUCAS: Sorry... Looks like this time I'm the one who...
MARIANA: Oh. It's you... You came at just the right moment.

(MARIANA kneels on the bed. LUCAS is disconcerted.)

LUCAS: No, don't scratch it.
MARIANA: But it itches...
LUCAS: It's worse if you scratch it.
MARIANA: But it feels so good.

(MARIANA scratches herself vigorously.)

LUCAS: You're going to hurt yourself.

MARIANA: I love scratching myself. I could scratch myself for hours and hours. I scratch and scratch myself... Come on, you scratch me.

LUCAS: Me? No. No, I can't... I don't know how.

MARIANA: Scratch me!

LUCAS: I'll put a little cream on you.

MARIANA: Yes, please.

(LUCAS opens the tube, squirts a little cream on his fingers and rubs it on the bite.)

MARIANA: More.

LUCAS: More?

MARIANA: It's just that it itches so much. So much.

(LUCAS goes back to rubbing MARIANA's thighs with great pleasure. MARIANA is apparently enjoying it.)

(DOMINGO knocks on the cabin door.)

(LUCAS stops what he's doing.)

LUCAS: Who is it?

(MARIANA gets up smiling and goes into the bathroom.)

DOMINGO: It's me. Domingo.

(LUCAS goes over and opens the door.)

DOMINGO: Have you seen my wife? *(LUCAS shakes his head.)* I don't know where she's got to, and I thought maybe she came for the cream.

(LUCAS gets the tube of cream off the bed and offers it to DOMINGO.)

(MARIANA appears outside the cabin. She crosses and lies down on the deckchair.)

LUCAS: Here you go.

DOMINGO: Thanks. I'll give it to her for you.

LUCAS: One application every four hours.
DOMINGO: Every four hours.
LUCAS: And make sure she doesn't scratch it.
DOMINGO: I should make sure.
LUCAS: If she scratches it, it'll get even more inflamed.
DOMINGO (*Skeptical*): I'll see what I can do. Goodbye.
LUCAS: Goodbye.

(*LUCAS closes the door and exits into the bathroom.*)

(*DOMINGO crosses towards the railing. He sees MARIANA and approaches her. He tosses her the tube of cream.*)

DOMINGO: Your cream.

(*MARIANA catches the cream and, after looking at it, leaves it on the deck.*)

DOMINGO: Are you still mad?
MARIANA: I don't know how I put up with you.

(*DOMINGO takes a pistol from his pocket and begins nonchalantly cleaning it off with a handkerchief.*)

MARIANA: What's that?
DOMINGO: What?
MARIANA: What you've got in your hand.
DOMINGO: This? A handkerchief. (*Pause.*) What did you think it was? A towel?

(*MARIANA lies back in the deckchair and puts on her sunglasses.*)

(*DOMINGO aims the pistol at her.*)

(*Pause.*)

MARIANA: It wouldn't be loaded?
DOMINGO: Give a little guess... (*DOMINGO makes a sudden turn and "fires" into the air.*) Pow! (*MARIANA jumps.*) Seagull soup for supper.

(*DOMINGO laughs at his joke. MARIANA gets up and tries to take the pistol from him.*)

MARIANA: You're driving me crazy!

(*They struggle. DOMINGO is egging her on. She stops.*)

DOMINGO: Why would it be loaded, woman? You think I'm crazy?

(*MARIANA goes into the cabin. DOMINGO picks up the tube of cream and follows her. He puts the pistol in his pocket.*)

(*MARIANA lies down on the bed. DOMINGO goes into the cabin. He sits down on a chair.*)

(*Pause.*)

(*DOMINGO has taken out his broken glasses and tries fixing them with some tape.*)

MARIANA: OK. I give up. (*Pause.*) If you didn't want me to come, why didn't you just tell me straight out?
DOMINGO: I didn't tell you straight out?
MARIANA: No.
DOMINGO: I didn't tell you that I should come down here first and then bring you down when I got settled in?
MARIANA: I thought that was just an opinion.
DOMINGO: Exactly. That was my opinion, and you turned up your nose at it.
MARIANA: Why can't we get settled in together?
DOMINGO: We can get settled in together. We can get settled in together, or we can get settled in one at a time. Which is what seems more reasonable to me.
MARIANA: That seems more reasonable to you?
DOMINGO: Yes.
MARIANA: Why?
DOMINGO: I told you why. I explained my reasons.
MARIANA: I don't understand.
DOMINGO: What is it you don't understand?
MARIANA: We're married. Why can't I come with you?

DOMINGO: I didn't say you couldn't come with me. I said I preferred to come on ahead. (*Pause.*) Mariana. Malabo is a hornet's nest. We've got us a thirteen million dollar black hole there. Every time I read the damned reports I just throw up my hands. And I don't know what I'm going to find there. Or more likely, I do know. A bunch of bald-faced crooks who've been lining their pockets as much as they can. Guinea isn't Spain, Mariana. It's not a country of law and order and legal systems. Its a military dictatorship where human life doesn't matter a damn. Where ordinary people have no defense against the whims of the people in power. And nobody's going to help me, because even if they wanted to, it wouldn't do any good. You understand? I'm going to have to swallow the whole crooked mess, and put on a big smile right and left, and not appear too bright if I don't want to wake up some morning with my balls in the garbage can.

(*Pause.*)

MARIANA: You've seen too many Tarzan movies.

(*Pause.*)

DOMINGO: I'm afraid for my balls, Mariana.
MARIANA: Then, why did you take the job?
DOMINGO: Why did I take the job?
MARIANA: Couldn't you have said no?
DOMINGO: And stay where I was.
MARIANA: Well, yes.
DOMINGO: It's a position of responsibility. A move up. Can't you understand that?

(*Pause.*)

MARIANA: What I can't understand is why you don't want me to come with you.
DOMINGO: What if something happens to you?
MARIANA: Nothing is going to happen to me. There are other women in Guinea. I checked it out.
DOMINGO: Other women?
MARIANA: Other Spanish women. Yes.
DOMINGO: Is that what's worrying you?

MARIANA: Don't make me laugh.

(*Pause.*)

DOMINGO: You think no one else ever looks at me?
MARIANA: I didn't say that.
DOMINGO: You don't think if I wanted to, I could find someone else?

(*Pause.*)

MARIANA: You're tired of me, aren't you?
DOMINGO: Sometimes.
MARIANA: Why don't you leave me then?
DOMINGO: Better a known evil...
MARIANA: You're a jerk.
DOMINGO: Why don't you leave me?
MARIANA: Is that what you want?

(*DOMINGO goes over to her. He sits on the bed.*)

DOMINGO: I want us to call a truce. We said in Guinea we were going to...
MARIANA: To start over.
DOMINGO: Right.
MARIANA: And starting over means me staying at home waiting till you get the urge to call me.
DOMINGO: Starting over means forgiving each other. (*Pause.*) I've forgiven you a lot of things. You know that. Now you forgive me.
MARIANA: Forgive what?
DOMINGO: My disappointing you. (*Pause.*) Maybe you'll know how to forgive me?

(*MARIANA embraces him. They kiss.*)

MARIANA: You haven't disappointed me.
DOMINGO: I haven't?
MARIANA: No. I'm the one who's disappointed you.
DOMINGO: We've both disappointed each other.
MARIANA: So I have disappointed you?

DOMINGO: I've disappointed you, you've disappointed me, he's disappointed himself, we've disappointed ourselves, you've disappointed yourselves, and they've disappointed themselves. (*Pause.*) Thirteen million dollars. (*Pause.*) How's your spider bite? (*DOMINGO tries to look at her thigh. MARIANA resists. They struggle playfully.*) Here it is... (*DOMINGO kisses her on the bite.*) Hmmm... tastes good...

MARIANA: Stop now...

DOMINGO: Your legs have not disappointed me...

MARIANA: Settle down now...

DOMINGO: Why?

MARIANA: We're talking...

DOMINGO: Fools rush in where talkers fear to tread. Down with talking, comrades, the time has come to act!

(*DOMINGO throws himself on her.*)

MARIANA: Domingo!

(*They roll around on the bed and fall on to the floor.*)

DOMINGO: Owww!

MARIANA: Domingo?

DOMINGO: Ow, ow, ow!

MARIANA: Did you hurt yourself?

DOMINGO: My arm... my elbow...

MARIANA: Let me see...

DOMINGO: What a stupid thing...

MARIANA: It's already swelling...

DOMINGO: Shit, shit, shit...

(*DOMINGO gets up and paces around anxiously holding his arm. MARIANA puts on a robe and goes to the door.*)

DOMINGO: What are you doing?

MARIANA: I'm going to get Lucas...

DOMINGO: Wait! (*MARIANA exits.*) Mariana! Mariana! Shit! Jesus H. fucking Christ!

(*MARIANA comes in followed by LUCAS who carries a small doctor's bag.*)

LUCAS: Let me see...
DOMINGO: Really, it's nothing...

(*LUCAS takes a look at the arm.*)

LUCAS: Can you make a fist? (*DOMINGO makes a fist.*) Move your arm...
DOMINGO: It hurts a little.
MARIANA: You've got a nice lump.
LUCAS: Looks like a sprain. It'll be better if you wrap it. (*He takes a bandage from his bag.*) At this rate you won't make it to Malabo. (*He wraps the arm.*) As soon as we hit port, you'd better get it x-rayed.
DOMINGO: It's probably nothing.
LUCAS: Just in case.

(*LUCAS finishes wrapping the arm.*)

DOMINGO: At least it's not my right arm. I can still let you get your revenge at ping-pong.
LUCAS: If it keeps hurting, let me know. I can give you a sedative. I'm afraid you might have a fracture.
MARIANA: We're imposing...
LUCAS: Come on. Just the opposite. The trip's turning out to be very entertaining. Do you feel any better?
DOMINGO: Thanks.
LUCAS: Good...
MARIANA: Let me get the door...
LUCAS: Don't worry. I know the way out.

(*Change in the cyclorama. Night. The ship's foghorn sounds.*)

(*DOMINGO knocks on the cabin door. LUCAS opens it.*)

DOMINGO: I think I could do with that sedative. I can't sleep a wink.
LUCAS: A bump like that can be painful. Sit down. (*DOMINGO sits. LUCAS looks at the arm.*) May I... Color isn't bad.

(*LUCAS takes out a vial and a syringe.*)

DOMINGO: I see you've got everything.
LUCAS: For the Mission. You know, illegal imports.

(*LUCAS prepares the injection.*)

DOMINGO: You spent much time in Africa?

LUCAS: Six years. You?

DOMINGO: No, first time for me. I'll be working for a while in Equatorial Guinea.

LUCAS: Joint operation?

DOMINGO: Sort of. I'll be coordinating Spanish foreign aid there.

LUCAS: Got it. The bureaucracy.

DOMINGO: Administration.

LUCAS: Roll up your sleeve. (*LUCAS gives DOMINGO an injection of sedative.*) So what are things like down there? I've heard it's a screwed up mess.

DOMINGO: Well, you understand, I'm not allowed to say. I haven't taken over yet.

LUCAS: If it's a state secret...

DOMINGO: You familiar with Guinea?

LUCAS: No, but from what I've seen of Black Africa, I can imagine it. If the French have left their part the way it is, ours must be like an old movie. Heart of darkness.

DOMINGO: You've read Conrad?

LUCAS: Love him.

DOMINGO: Me too. But scarey. Makes your skin crawl. (*LUCAS tosses the syringe in the wastebasket.*) Anyway, I suppose Africa has changed since then.

LUCAS: Very little.

DOMINGO: You think?

LUCAS: Don't expect to find anything else. You want a beer?

DOMINGO: Won't that be bad with the...?

LUCAS: You rather have a coke?

DOMINGO: I'd rather have a beer. (*LUCAS gets two beers from a cooler. Opens them.*) Don't you miss Spain?

LUCAS: I go back every year for a spell. Besides, we're all Spanish at the mission. Because of the malaria.

DOMINGO: Because of the malaria?

LUCAS: It's endemic down there. It seems the Iberian Peninsula was a malarial zone until recently, relatively speaking. We carry the antibodies. So we're the Europeans with the best resistance. Advantages of underdevelopment.

DOMINGO: Listen. What about AIDS?

LUCAS: Well, for that, the fewer antibodies we have, the better.

DOMINGO: No, I mean, is there a lot of it? I've heard the Blacks are very promiscuous.

LUCAS: They're more spontaneous than we are.

DOMINGO: More spontaneous?

LUCAS: A lot more. I could tell you things that...

DOMINGO: You?... Anthropologically speaking, you mean?

LUCAS: Their attitude towards sex is a lot purer than ours.

DOMINGO: Purer?

LUCAS: Healthier, more... innocent.

DOMINGO: And you approve of that?

LUCAS: Of course.

DOMINGO: Good God!

(Pause. Suddenly a torrential rain. LUCAS and DOMINGO watch silently as the rain falls.)

LUCAS: It just comes out of nowhere. When you least expect it. And as fast as it comes, it's gone. Life is like that here. Nature imposing its mood. It's not like in the city where you hardly notice the rain or a dry spell. It's something of no importance; you turn on the faucet, and the water always comes out. And it comes out clean. And it's worth nothing. The dirtier water is the more it's worth. Man turns everything into something artificial, something manufactured, i.e., something insignificant. And people's lives stop having value too. They just occur, one after another with no one noticing. Life occurs and no one notices. That's the bad thing about cities. Nothing means anything. In Africa life shows itself off every day. I've learned to recognize its presence: the happiness of water, the strength of the sun, the weight of darkness. Genuine darkness where things become uncertain and turn into shadows that question us.

(LUCAS notices that DOMINGO has fallen asleep on the bed. He stops talking and drinks his beer.)

(MARIANA knocks on the door of the cabin. LUCAS goes to open it.)

(The storm has ended. LUCAS opens the door.)

MARIANA: Is Domingo with you? *(LUCAS invites her in. MARIANA sees DOMINGO asleep on the bed.)* Did something happen?

LUCAS: He's asleep.
MARIANA: Yes, but...
LUCAS: Let him sleep. He needs it.
MARIANA: What about you?

(*LUCAS shrugs his shoulders.*)

LUCAS: I'm not sleepy.

(*MARIANA looks at the sleeping DOMINGO. She turns off the lamp on the nightstand.*)

MARIANA: When he's asleep, he looks like a little boy. He gets smaller.

(*MARIANA sits on the bed next to DOMINGO.*)

LUCAS: Do you have children?

(*Pause. MARIANA gets up.*)

MARIANA: What brought on that question?
LUCAS: I'm sorry. (*Pause. MARIANA sits down next to LUCAS.*) That was out of line.
MARIANA: You don't have to apologize. (*Pause.*) We've never had the time. That's the only problem. We haven't found the right moment. (*Pause.*) We haven't learned how to find the right moment.

(*Pause.*)

LUCAS: It's something that happens to a lot of people.
MARIANA: What's that matter to me? There are blind people and cripples too, but that doesn't make me jump for joy.
LUCAS: Sorry.

(*Pause.*)

MARIANA: But you're right. It's like rats. You know when rats don't have enough space, they stop reproducing, naturally? The females stop being fertile until the population decreases.

(*Pause.*)

LUCAS: I'm sorry.
MARIANA: Why are you always saying you're sorry?
LUCAS: Me?

(*Pause. MARIANA picks up DOMINGO's beer and takes a sip. LUCAS looks at his shoes.*)

MARIANA: I feel as if I've closed my eyes, and ten years have passed.
LUCAS: You're tired.

(*MARIANA nods agreement.*)

MARIANA: Do you want to sleep on my bed?
LUCAS: Don't worry about it.
MARIANA: I'm not worried.

(*MARIANA gets up and leaves the cabin.*)

(*MARIANA leaning on the railing. LUCAS exits from the cabin. He goes up to her. Pause. The sound of music from a distance.*)

MARIANA: How deceitful you are.
LUCAS: Deceitful?
MARIANA: Yes.
LUCAS: No more than the average guy.
MARIANA: Very deceitful.
LUCAS: That's the average guy?
MARIANA: Yes.
LUCAS: If I am, I'm not aware of it.
MARIANA: You're so deceitful you manage to believe yourself. (*MARIANA draws him into dancing. Pause.*) Have you ever had the feeling that you've left something unsaid? (*LUCAS looks at her.*) It's sad. And then you regret it.
LUCAS: Is there something you've left unsaid?
MARIANA: I like you. (*They continue dancing.*) There, you see. Now I feel better.
LUCAS: I like you too.

(*Pause.*)

MARIANA: Aren't you going to kiss me?
LUCAS: I don't want to.
MARIANA: You don't want to?
LUCAS: Is it obligatory?
MARIANA: Yes.
LUCAS: What for?
MARIANA: What for?
LUCAS: It would lead to nothing.
MARIANA: It has to lead to something?
LUCAS: Isn't that important to you?
MARIANA: It's most important. (*They dance.*)   Are you in love?
LUCAS: No. (*Pause.*) I don't want to. (*Pause.*) I don't want to fall in love.
   (*Pause.*) I don't want to suffer.

(*Pause.*)

MARIANA: Don't be afraid.

(*They kiss passionately. DOMINGO appears with pistol in hand. He fires. Blackout. Torrential downpour.*)

(*The light in the bathroom is on. MARIANA sits up in bed.*)

MARIANA: Domingo?

(*DOMINGO comes out of the bathroom and starts undressing.*)

DOMINGO: Go back to sleep.
MARIANA: What are you doing?
DOMINGO: Going to bed.
MARIANA: What time is it?
DOMINGO: Very late. (*Pause.*) Or very early. Depending on how you look
   at it.

(*DOMINGO crawls into bed.*)

MARIANA: You're freezing.
DOMINGO: I'm dead.

Travesía. Príncipe Gran Vía Theater, Madrid, 1993.
Directed by Fermín Cabal. Luisa Martínez. Photo: Chicho.

MARIANA: How's your arm?

DOMINGO: I don't know. I must have left it around here somewhere, because I can't feel it. (*Pause.*) I don't know what shit that turkey gave me, but it did me in roundly. You're going to laugh. All of a sudden I wake up and find myself in bed with him. Scared the shit out of me.

MARIANA: Why?

DOMINGO: What do you mean, why? I'm not in the habit of sleeping with men. Of course it must seem normal to you. You've had more experience.

MARIANA: Very funny... Let go of me.

DOMINGO: I just want to get warm. (*Pause.*) Mariana, don't start with the feminist crap.

MARIANA: Will you settle down!

DOMINGO: Ow! You hit my bad arm...

MARIANA: Next time I'll hit some place worse.

(*LUCAS leans on the rail looking out to sea. Change in the cyclorama. Day.*)

(*DOMINGO comes over to him. He also leans on the railing. He is wearing his arm in a sling.*)

DOMINGO: Magnificent morning. Promising.

LUCAS: Did you sleep well?

DOMINGO: I needed it. I have to thank you. That sedative of yours had a fantastic effect.

LUCAS: You were worn out.

DOMINGO: Well, I needed it.

LUCAS: Seeing things a lot clearer now?

DOMINGO: Maybe. (*Pause.*) The clearer I see things the darker they look. (*Pause.*) I ask myself what the hell I'm doing here.

LUCAS: On the boat?

DOMINGO: In Africa. I don't think I'm cut out for this. I don't fit the pattern of Conrad's heros.

LUCAS: Why did you come then?

DOMINGO: Phufff!... It's a long story. And embarrassing. (*Pause.*) But you have experience with these things. Maybe you could give me some advice. That's your line of work, isn't it?

LUCAS: What's that?

DOMINGO: A shepherd of souls. Isn't that how they say it? Well, so here you've got a poor, little, tormented lamb ready for confession.
LUCAS: I think you've made a mistake. I'm not a priest.
DOMINGO: You're not? What are you, a lay brother?
LUCAS: Just a plain old sheep, like you.
DOMINGO: Aren't you a missionary?
LUCAS: Secular, if you want to call it that. I work in the Mission at Mopti, as a nurse. That's it.

(*Pause.*)

DOMINGO: Well, you're missing a great story. You haven't seen my wife?
LUCAS: No.
DOMINGO: Sleeping in I guess.
LUCAS: She got to bed pretty late last night.
DOMINGO: Really?
LUCAS: We got to talking and lost track of the time.
DOMINGO: Don't tell me. I get the picture. You'll have had your fill already of listening to personal problems. Good. I won't take up any more of your time.

(*DOMINGO goes off toward the cabin.*)

(*DOMINGO enters the cabin. He is still wearing his arm in a sling. MARIANA is sleeping. DOMINGO lets in the light. MARIANA wakes up.*)

MARIANA: You scared me.
DOMINGO: I scared you? That'll be the day.
MARIANA: I had a nightmare. I was in the bed I had when I was a little girl, and all of a sudden a man came in with a pistol and killed me.
DOMINGO: You must have done something. Who was he?
MARIANA: I think my father. I don't know. I'm not sure.
DOMINGO: Then why do say your father?
MARIANA: I don't know.
DOMINGO: Get dressed. We need to talk.
MARIANA: I can't talk in bed?
DOMINGO: Just get dressed.

(*MARIANA gets out of bed.*)

MARIANA: Can I take a shower?

(DOMINGO doesn't answer. MARIANA goes into the bathroom. DOMINGO sits down next to the nightstand. He picks up the Conquest of the Atlantic book which is on the stand.)

(In the bathroom water is heard running.)

(DOMINGO puts the book down and goes over to the bathroom door. He looks in.)

DOMINGO: You're getting fat.

(The water stops running.)

MARIANA *(Off)*: One time he beat up my mother.
DOMINGO: Was she a whore too?

(Pause. MARIANA comes out of the bathroom wrapped in a towel.)

MARIANA: What's the matter with you?
DOMINGO: We need to talk.
MARIANA: Well then, talk.

(MARIANA goes back into the bathroom.)

DOMINGO: Mariana, I want to tell you a story that will interest you. You know Angel Mora's secretary?
MARIANA *(Off)*: The short dumpy thing with the frizzy hair?
DOMINGO: She's not that short.
MARIANA *(Off)*: A little dippy, kind of a nothing...
DOMINGO: That's the one.
MARIANA *(Off)*: So, what about her?
DOMINGO: I've screwed her.

(MARIANA comes out of the bathroom. They look at each other.)

MARIANA: Should I congratulate you?
DOMINGO: One afternoon when I was working on some report that I had to finish up or else, Angel asked her to give me a hand.

MARIANA: And she took him literally.

DOMINGO: I was just looking at her. She's a very good looking woman. I mean, we have to admit our friend has good taste.

(*MARIANA watches him attentively.*)

DOMINGO: She glanced up at me, and I just kept looking at her. We just looked at each other for a while, and then we did it, right there. On the floor.

MARIANA: The perfect secretary. You should recommend her for a promotion.

DOMINGO: She told me she was going through a pretty intense personal crisis since Angel had thrown her over for someone else. (*Pause.*) And then she told me who someone else was. (*Pause.*) Poor little fool probably thought screwing me would be some kind of revenge for her. As if you'd give a damn. (*Pause.*) Imagine how I felt when that son of a bitch calls me into his office a few days later. "Domingo! How's it going, Domingo?" And he tells me the good news that he wants me to take charge of the Bank of Guinea. (*Pause.*) Finding out about your affair with Angel had hurt, but I was managing it. A cuckold's horns are like antennae; he always ends up sensing something going on. And I mean, it even made me feel easier knowing the truth. But when that cynical bastard had the gall to get me out of the way like that, I lost it. I told him I'd have to consult with you. I got out to the street, and I started walking. And all of a sudden I felt completely calm. I opened my eyes and saw some young kid waiting for the bus. "Where am I?" I said. He smiled and said, "In Madrid." I thought it was funny, too. I caught a taxi, went back to the office, and accepted. (*Pause.*) I felt like I was coming out of a tunnel. (*Pause.*) Like I was starting all over again. (*Pause.*) Until you said you wanted to come with me.

(*Pause.*)

MARIANA: There's just one piece of information you're missing. I was the one who asked Angel to offer you an overseas post.

DOMINGO: In Guinea.

MARIANA: Wherever.

DOMINGO: And that son of a bitch sends me to Guinea.

MARIANA: I wanted to start all over again, too. To erase the whole surrounding landscape. To stop seeing the faces of all those happy idiots around us. To haul ass out of here and try to do something different for once in our life.

DOMINGO: To do what?

MARIANA: I don't know. I have some plans for when we get to Malabo. I want to do my part, Domingo. I'm not asking for more than that.

DOMINGO: Don't make me laugh. A week after we get there you'll be playing tennis and throwing yourself at the first available hunk.

(*Pause.*)

MARIANA: Give me a chance.

(*Pause.*)

DOMINGO: Have you already thrown yourself at him?

MARIANA: Domingo.

DOMINGO: Answer me.

MARIANA: I don't know what you're talking about.

DOMINGO: What did you do last night?

MARIANA: We talked.

DOMINGO: Did you go looking for him, or did he come here?

MARIANA: I went looking for you. Because you didn't come back.

DOMINGO: And you said: well, since we're here anyway...

MARIANA: He's a priest, Domingo.

DOMINGO: He's a nothing. And you know it. Don't give me that crap. (*Pause.*) It's over. As soon as we get off the boat, you go back to Madrid. On this same boat if you're afraid to take a plane. In the meantime, Mariana, don't play with fire. Don't forget I've got a gun. You hear me? I don't have anything more to say.

(*MARIANA leaves the cabin.*)

(*MARIANA at the railing. She sits in a deckchair. She rubs on suntan lotion. LUCAS enters. He leans on the railing.*)

(*Pause.*)

(*LUCAS looks over at MARIANA.*)

LUCAS: Good morning. (*MARIANA doesn't answer. LUCAS goes over to her.*) Mind if I sit down?
MARIANA: They're not mine.

(*LUCAS sits on a deckchair.*)

LUCAS: Are you angry about something?
MARIANA: Why didn't you tell me you weren't a priest?
LUCAS: I didn't tell you I was.

(*Pause.*)

MARIANA: You knew that I thought you were.
LUCAS: I'm not a mind-reader.
MARIANA: Right.

(*Pause.*)

LUCAS: I didn't say I was.
MARIANA: I heard you already.
LUCAS: Is it so important?
MARIANA: Not at all.

(*Pause.*)

LUCAS: All right. I admit it. At one point I did think that you might have made that mistake. But I didn't think it was important. (*Pause.*) I kind of enjoyed it. I was afraid if it got cleared up, our relationship wouldn't be so easy.
MARIANA: What relationship?
LUCAS: I kind of enjoyed just talking with you. (*Pause.*) If I had told you, would you have stayed with me the other night?
MARIANA: I suppose so. I kind of enjoyed it, too.
LUCAS: What difference does it make then?
MARIANA: You didn't let me do the deciding.
LUCAS: I'm sorry.
MARIANA (*Mocking him*): I'm sorry.
LUCAS: OK. I'm not sorry. I did what I felt like. And I don't think it's that big a deal.

(Pause. DOMINGO appears side stage. He is wearing his arm in a sling. He watches them.)

MARIANA: I feel tired. Just leave me alone.
LUCAS: I'm sorry... Oh, excuse me!... Phuffff!

(LUCAS gets up and starts to leave. He discovers DOMINGO next to the ping-pong table.)

DOMINGO: A little game?
LUCAS: No, thanks.

(DOMINGO goes over to MARIANA. He sits down.)

DOMINGO: Change of serve. *(Pause.)* What were you talking about?
MARIANA: Nothing.
DOMINGO: Your favorite subject.
MARIANA: Will you all just leave me in peace?
DOMINGO: We all? Is there someone else here? *(MARIANA gets up and starts off.)* Where are you going?

(MARIANA exits. DOMINGO reclines on the deckchair. He takes out the pistol and plays with it.)

(LUCAS enters. They look at each other.)

DOMINGO: You like firearms?
LUCAS: No.
DOMINGO: They say they're necessary in Africa.
LUCAS: For what?
DOMINGO: For getting respect. You know: the cross in one hand and the sword in the other.
LUCAS: If I were you I wouldn't make a big show of it.
DOMINGO: No?
LUCAS: I think they're going to have you for lunch.
DOMINGO: Ugh. Nice thought. Are there still cannibals?

(LUCAS exits.)

(DOMINGO remains by the railing, smiling. He takes out a flask and drinks.)

(LUCAS enters the cabin where MARIANA is sitting.)

LUCAS: What are you doing here?
MARIANA: I wanted to apologize.
LUCAS: You?
MARIANA: I have my weaknesses too.
LUCAS: You picked a bad moment. You husband is walking around with a pistol.
MARIANA: Are you afraid?
LUCAS: It's not part of my plan to get shot for some foolishness.

(MARIANA smiles.)

MARIANA: Then close the door. *(LUCAS looks at her without saying anything.)* Close it.

(On deck DOMINGO suddenly lets out a scream.)

DOMINGO: Ahhhhhhhhhh!

(DOMINGO exits running and enters the cabin. He turns on the light. MARIANA is on the bed. She looks at him.)

DOMINGO: Where did you get to?
MARIANA: Here.
DOMINGO: I've looked all over the boat for you.
MARIANA: I was in the dining room.

(Pause.)

DOMINGO: Did you go to his cabin?
MARIANA: I don't have to give you an accounting...
DOMINGO: Did you or didn't you?
MARIANA: No!

(DOMINGO goes off in a fury.)

(LUCAS comes out of the bathroom brushing his teeth. He sees MARIANA sitting in the room.)

LUCAS: What are you doing here?
MARIANA: Can you help me?
LUCAS: Say the word.
MARIANA: Domingo's acting like a crazy man. He thinks something's going on between us.
LUCAS: And?
MARIANA: Couldn't you talk to him?
LUCAS: Me? If he thinks that, I'm the last person...
MARIANA: Shhhhh! Lower your voice.

(Pause.)

LUCAS: Anyway, for your own peace of mind, I'll tell you we arrive in Akra tomorrow.
MARIANA: Tomorrow?
LUCAS: At dawn, apparently.
MARIANA: You didn't tell me that.
LUCAS: You know I like to keep things from you. *(Pause. DOMINGO knocks on the cabin door.)*   Who is it?

(MARIANA makes signs not to open it.)

DOMINGO *(Outside)*: It's me!
LUCAS: The door's open.

(To LUCAS's dismay MARIANA crawls under the bed. DOMINGO enters.)

DOMINGO: Is Mariana here?

(LUCAS, disconcerted and toothbrush in hand, just looks at him.)

LUCAS: I was brushing my teeth.
DOMINGO: It's just that I can't find her.
LUCAS: Don't worry. She can't go very far.

(Pause.)

DOMINGO: You have an aspirin? I've got a slight headache.
LUCAS: You want a valium?
DOMINGO: A valium?
LUCAS: You seem a little nervous.
DOMINGO: A little seasick again, that's all.
LUCAS: Keep taking those pills.
DOMINGO: I will. You're right.
LUCAS: Have you eaten anything yet?
DOMINGO: I don't have any appetite.
LUCAS: Still, you ought to eat something. You'll feel better.
DOMINGO: Yea, maybe so... I won't bother you.
LUCAS: You don't want the aspirin?
DOMINGO: No. That's OK.

(*DOMINGO leaves the cabin.*)

(*Pause. MARIANA sticks her head out from under the bed.*)

LUCAS: What are you waiting for?

(*MARIANA gets out from under the bed.*)

MARIANA: I owe you one. You probably saved my life. According to the law of the jungle, I'm in your hands.
LUCAS: You don't owe me anything. I did it for myself. (*Pause.*) It'd probably be better if you left now.
MARIANA: I'm afraid to be with him.
LUCAS: Why don't you leave him?

(*Pause.*)

MARIANA: I should have done it already, but it's not so simple. You hold on to the illusion that it's possible to change things. But it's already decided. We've reached the end. (*Pause.*) I expected so much from this trip. To get to know Africa. A whole different world.
LUCAS: Don't create more illusions. Did you read the book I lent you? A knowledge of Africa is always superficial. Just trading along the coast. It's difficult getting to the interior. It took the French a hundred and fifty years to get to Timbuktu. It got to where they didn't think it existed; it was a myth like Eldorado. In fact, it's easier to think that Africa doesn't

exist, that it's not any part of humanity. There's something in the Black race that makes it impossible to accept. A European, an Arab, a Chinese, or a Malay can be different, but they're part of a continuum; there are undeniable resemblances, features in common. But not so the Black. The Black is burnt, the American Indians say, and they find it disgusting to touch them. Of course there are Whites who come to feel affection for Blacks, who even come to love them. But I ask myself, isn't it perhaps the kind of affection you feel for an animal? Aren't there people who love a cat more than they love a person begging on the street corner?

MARIANA: You're joking.

LUCAS: Blacks, for White people, are like animals. At best, like an animal who's loved. And like every animal, the possibility always exists that he'll turn savage. After all, that would be quite natural: one day he throws himself on us and sinks those big, white teeth into our leg.

MARIANA: What you're saying is horrible.

LUCAS: But it's true.

MARIANA: Are you a racist?

LUCAS: What do you mean by a racist?

MARIANA: Believing one race is superior to another.

LUCAS: Then I'm a racist. I believe Blacks are superior to us. But unfortunately I'm White, and I can't do anything about it. I could get sunburned till I'm black as coal, but even then, I doubt if I could understand what it is to be a Black man. (*Pause.*) And don't think I haven't tried.

(*Pause.*)

MARIANA: So, why are you there?

LUCAS: I'm happy in Mopti. (*Pause.*) You end up doing what you've prepared yourself to do. Everything I'm doing now I used to dream about before. I'm comfortable with it, and I find it meaningful. And I can grow with it, and everyday I get better at doing more things. (*Pause.*) I like the feeling of being good at things. (*Pause.*) I owe a lot to Africa. It's taught me important things. I don't say I've learned them well. That's another matter. But it's taught me them.

MARIANA: Like what?

(*Pause.*)

LUCAS: Not to expect anything in order to be happy.

MARIANA: I don't understand.

LUCAS: Don't you want to be happy? (*MARIANA nods agreement.*) Well, for that you have to be able not to expect anything. (*Pause.*) It's not easy. You have to start by learning to be alone.

MARIANA: And then?

LUCAS: I don't know. I'm still at that point.

(*Pause.*)

MARIANA: I don't know if I understand you, but... No, no, I don't understand you. But I envy you. You're strong.

LUCAS: Me?

MARIANA: You're sure of yourself.

LUCAS: Me?

MARIANA: Because you believe in things. (*Pause.*) Me, I'm the opposite, I'm full of... panic. Maybe I haven't learned to be alone. (*Pause.*) We may not see each other again. (*Pause.*) Have you ever had the feeling that you've left something unsaid? (*LUCAS looks at her.*) And later you regret it.

(*Pause.*)

LUCAS: You can't always say everything.

(*Pause.*)

MARIANA: No, of course. Not everything. (*Pause.*) I have to go. (*Pause.*) Goodbye.

LUCAS: Goodbye.

(*MARIANA crosses toward the door.*)

LUCAS: Mariana.

MARIANA: Yes?

(*LUCAS goes to her. He takes off his Tuareg necklace and offers it to her.*)

LUCAS: Can I give you a gift?

(*Pause.*)

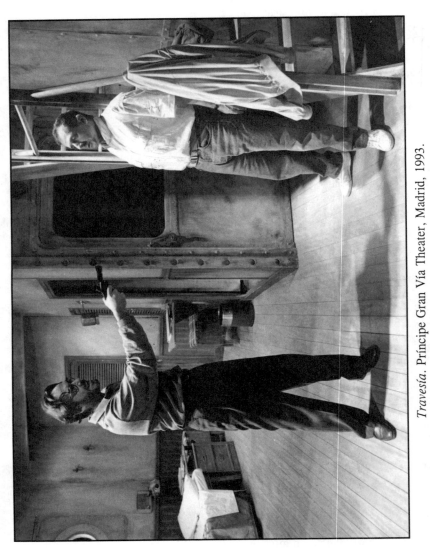

Travesía. Príncipe Gran Vía Theater, Madrid, 1993.
Directed by Fermín Cabal. Santiago Ramos and Emilio Gutiérrez Caba. Photo: Chicho.

MARIANA: I don't accept gifts. (*Pause.*) I also have my pride.

(*MARIANA exits from the cabin.*)

(*DOMINGO is at the railing with his arm in a sling. He takes a flask of whisky from his jacket pocket. He drinks a long slug.*)

(*LUCAS enters and sees him drinking.*)

DOMINGO: A drink?

(*LUCAS takes the flask, wipes the top, drinks, and returns it.*)

LUCAS: I was looking for you.
DOMINGO: You want your revenge match?
LUCAS: You're not in any condition.
DOMINGO: One hand's more than I need to beat you.
LUCAS: Let's brag a little!
DOMINGO: Not bragging. In ping-pong that's all you need. But if you want, I'll let you hit it with both hands.
LUCAS: You're an imbecile.
DOMINGO: I don't strike you as a nice guy. (*Pause.*) You prefer my wife, right?
LUCAS: You're about to lose her.
DOMINGO: Well, now's your chance.
LUCAS: She's a good woman.
DOMINGO: Oh, you've had a sample? I thought so.

(*DOMINGO takes another drink.*)

LUCAS: You're drunk.
DOMINGO: Want some? (*LUCAS refuses the offer.*) She has a nice ass, don't you think? (*Pause.*) And gives great head. (*Pause.*) Don't tell me she hasn't sucked it for you? My God, man, what've you been doing? She's a real artist! Next to her Titian and El Greco are just beginners. The Prado's a shithouse.

(*LUCAS collars him violently. He raises the bottle.*)

LUCAS: And you're a real bastard!

(DOMINGO laughs.)

DOMINGO: I don't deny it. What do you want me to say?

(LUCAS lets go of him.)

LUCAS: I'm going to ask her to come with me.
DOMINGO: You don't know what you're getting yourself into.
LUCAS: I'll take that chance.

(LUCAS turns his back on him to go. DOMINGO pulls out the pistol.)

DOMINGO: Stop right there! *(LUCAS turns around. They look at each other.)* If you go near her again, I'll kill you.
LUCAS: Then kill me now.
DOMINGO: Your move first.
LUCAS: You're a coward.
DOMINGO: But I'm crazy, don't forget.
LUCAS: They'll put you away.
DOMINGO: And they'll bury you. I'll win.
LUCAS: You're playing with an advantage.
DOMINGO: I'm the injured party, right? My choice of weapons.
LUCAS: But I don't have a weapon.

(Pause.)

DOMINGO *(Indicating the ping-pong table)*: I'll play you for her.

(Pause.)

LUCAS: Ping-pong?
DOMINGO: Like two gentlemen. Like Englishmen.
LUCAS: I'm not an Englishman.
DOMINGO: But you're a gentleman, right? *(Pressing the pistol to LUCAS's throat.)* If you lose, you shut yourself up in your cabin and we don't see a hair of you. If you win... *(Making a reverential bow.)*
LUCAS: OK.
DOMINGO: OK. Choose your racket.

(DOMINGO examines the rackets. He selects one. LUCAS takes the other one and looks it over. He warms up with a little wrist movement. He takes off his jacket and rolls up his sleeves. DOMINGO wipes off the table with his handkerchief. Then he tries out the imaginary ball.)

DOMINGO: A little warm-up?
LUCAS: No need.
DOMINGO: To eleven?
LUCAS: And volley for serve.
DOMINGO: OK. Volley for serve.

(DOMINGO puts the ball in play. LUCAS returns it. DOMINGO likewise. LUCAS slams it. LUCAS's point.)

DOMINGO *(Chasing the ball)*: No. Damn it. It has to go over four times.
LUCAS: What?
DOMINGO: It has to go over the net four times before it's in play.
LUCAS: But it went over four times. One, two, three, and four.
DOMINGO: You won on the third hit. Has to be four.
LUCAS: OK. Serve again.
DOMINGO: No. You serve.

(DOMINGO throws him the ball. LUCAS serves. DOMINGO returns. LUCAS likewise. DOMINGO hits it again.)

DOMINGO: And four... *(LUCAS slams it for the point. DOMINGO recovers the ball. He is not able to hide his annoyance.)* This time, yes. And by the rules.

(LUCAS takes the ball. He prepares to serve.)

LUCAS: Ready?
DOMINGO: Ready.

(LUCAS serves for the point. DOMINGO throws the ball back.)

LUCAS: Ready?
DOMINGO: Ready.

(LUCAS serves for another point. DOMINGO throws the ball back.)

LUCAS: Ready?
DOMINGO: Ready damnit.

(*LUCAS serves a point. DOMINGO throws back the ball. LUCAS motions that he's going to serve. DOMINGO OK's. LUCAS serves. On the tenth hit DOMINGO knocks it wide. LUCAS chases after the ball.*)

DOMINGO (*Untying the sling on his bad arm*): Three, love.

(*LUCAS goes to serve but stops.*)

LUCAS: Four.
DOMINGO: What do you mean, four?
LUCAS: Four, love.
DOMINGO: You sure?
LUCAS: Very sure.
DOMINGO: If you say so... We're among gentlemen.
LUCAS: Ready?
DOMINGO: Ready.

(*LUCAS serves. On the sixth hit DOMINGO slams a point. LUCAS goes after the ball. DOMINGO takes off his jacket and downs a swig from his flask. LUCAS throws him the ball.*)

DOMINGO: Four, one. My serve. (*DOMINGO serves. LUCAS returns and faults.*) Four, two. (*DOMINGO gets the ball. He serves and LUCAS nets the ball.*) And four, three. Pay attention to the game.
LUCAS (*Throws him the ball*): Serve.

(*DOMINGO serves. On the sixth hit the ball trips over the net, and DOMINGO fails to get to it.*)

DOMINGO: Give me a break, ace. (*Throwing back the ball.*) Fucking net.
LUCAS: Five, three.

(*DOMINGO serves and, on the fifth hit, takes the point.*)

DOMINGO: Five, four. And my serve, friend.

(*DOMINGO attempts a difficult serve. LUCAS makes a hard return and takes the point.*)

LUCAS: Not bad, huh?
DOMINGO: Change courts.
LUCAS: What?
DOMINGO: Mid-match. Change courts.

(*They change positions around the table.*)

LUCAS: Where's the ball?
DOMINGO: Over there. At the foot of the stairs. (*LUCAS retrieves the ball and serves. Faults.*) Fault. (*Throws him the ball. LUCAS serves again and faults.*) And double fault. Fucking sun in your face, huh?
LUCAS: Doesn't bother me.

(*DOMINGO throws the ball back.*)

DOMINGO: Six, five.

(*LUCAS serves. Hitting back and forth. LUCAS takes charge and has DOMINGO scrambling from side to side. On the ninth hit DOMINGO loses his balance and falls to the deck.*)

LUCAS: You hurt yourself? (*DOMINGO's leg is hurt from the fall. LUCAS doesn't see this from the other side of the table and comes around toward him, concerned. DOMINGO struggles up, holding his leg. He takes the pistol out of his pants pocket.*) What's the matter?
DOMINGO: The pistol... Dug into my thigh. (*DOMINGO puts the pistol on the table for a moment. LUCAS jumps on it. They struggle. LUCAS gets hold of the pistol. DOMINGO tries to grab him again, but LUCAS gets away and puts the table between them.*) You're not a gentleman.

(*LUCAS unloads the pistol and throws the bullets overboard.*)

LUCAS: Enough of that nonsense.

(*LUCAS puts the pistol in his pocket. Pause.*)

DOMINGO: Was that good?

LUCAS: What?
DOMINGO: That last point?
LUCAS: I think it was in.
DOMINGO: Then we're tied.
LUCAS: The game's over.
DOMINGO: You're not going to play anymore?
LUCAS: Of course not.
DOMINGO: Then I didn't get beat.
LUCAS: Can you walk?
DOMINGO: Perfectly.

(*DOMINGO takes a few steps towards the cabin. He staggers, and LUCAS grabs him.*)

LUCAS: Let me help you.
DOMINGO: You!!... You?... Don't make me laugh... I see already how you help me. Brother Lucas, my brother in Christ and in the Holy Virgin Mary, who, since you got on this boat, have been thinking of nothing but throwing yourself at my wife! But, of course, you're doing it out of love. Big words: love, loyalty, friendship... But love, love who? Love me, brother Lucas? Or love that dimwit little whore who lives off of my hard work, little brother?... Her, so feminist, so postmodern, so versed in the trendiest trend, but she lives off my hard work,... she eats up the profits, strips me of the plus-value. You know what plus-value is? Right, fuck, like you're going to know... Me, I'm up to my ass with the big words. I'm going to explode from all the big words!... Love! Love of yourself! Like everybody else!

(*LUCAS has given him up for impossible. He has gone toward the ping-pong table and picked up his jacket. He watches DOMINGO who continues his jabbering, while staggering about. LUCAS follows him picking up DOMINGO's jacket and the whisky flask and then comes up to him.*)

LUCAS: What you're going to explode from is the booze you're full of.
DOMINGO: You don't want to hear me, do you?
LUCAS: I have been hearing you long enough, and all you're saying are big words.
DOMINGO: Me? So now I'm the one who's saying the big words...

LUCAS: I don't know what you're saying anymore. And I doubt if you do.

DOMINGO: I just want a little corner. Is that so much to ask? A little corner in this fucking world where I can breathe easy. Because I'm up to my neck in shit. Up to my neck! I look around and what do I see? A swarm of arrogant bastards slugging it out to take over the store, like flies around a bucket of shit. They talk about democracy, and freedom, and decency... And they're biting each other to death to see who can get his hand in first! That is Spain, my dear friend. That is the world!

LUCAS: And you take it out on your wife.

DOMINGO: What? What'd you say?

LUCAS: You heard me.

DOMINGO: I'm only asking for something clean... Something pure! You won't know what that is either...

LUCAS: I confess I don't.

(*DOMINGO takes the flask and jacket from him. He starts off toward the cabin.*)

DOMINGO: A little something pure.

(*DOMINGO exits. Change on the cyclorama. Night.*)

(*LUCAS is packing his suitcase in the cabin.*)

(*MARIANA knocks at the door.*)

LUCAS: Who is it?

(*MARIANA opens the door and steps in. They look at each other.*)

MARIANA: Domingo says you two played ping-pong for me.

LUCAS: He was drunk.

MARIANA: Who was?

LUCAS: He was.

MARIANA: You didn't play?

LUCAS: With a pistol pointed at me.

MARIANA: You did play. (*Pause.*) Don't you think the match was a little unequal? You never played before. He was the only one who could win.

LUCAS: What?

MARIANA: Whatever the bet was. (*Pause.*) What if you had won?

LUCAS: What?
MARIANA: Would you have taken me with you?
LUCAS: Would you want to come with me?
MARIANA: Is that an offer?
LUCAS: It's an invitation. Didn't you want to get to know Africa?
MARIANA: You say that's impossible.

(*Pause.*)

LUCAS: Come with me.
MARIANA: But you didn't win the match.
LUCAS: Does one have to win it?
MARIANA: To be entitled.
LUCAS: You're right. (*Pause. LUCAS takes the pistol out of his pocket.*)
  You like the idea of Russian Roulette? (*LUCAS puts the pistol to his
  temple.*) Will you say yes?

(*Pause.*)

MARIANA: Don't be stupid. (*MARIANA tries to take away the pistol. They
  struggle for a second, and LUCAS lets it go.*) Have you gone crazy too?
LUCAS: It's not loaded. (*LUCAS asks for the pistol, and MARIANA gives it
  to him.*) Makes you realize the power a pistol has, doesn't it?

(*A dull knock on the door. LUCAS and MARIANA look at each other.*)

DOMINGO (*Outside*): Mariana! Mariana!
LUCAS: Are you going to get under the bed?
MARIANA: It's not necessary. (*MARIANA goes to the door.*) What do you
  want?
DOMINGO (*Outside*): I'm dying.

(*MARIANA and LUCAS look at each other. MARIANA opens the door.
On opening, DOMINGO falls through heavily and to the floor. LUCAS
throws the pistol on the bed and goes to help him.*)

MARIANA: What have you done?
DOMINGO: I took those pills... My stomach's burning up.
MARIANA: What pills?
DOMINGO: All of them.

MARIANA: Which ones?
DOMINGO: All of them. I just told you...

(*LUCAS gets him up, MARIANA helping.*)

LUCAS: Get him to the bathroom, quick! (*They go off to the bathroom. From off-stage*) Get rid of it! All of it! (*Noises in the bathroom. Water from a faucet. DOMINGO being sick.*) Stick your fingers down his throat!

(*DOMINGO is vomiting loudly. The sounds of DOMINGO begin to fuse with the sounds of the ocean.*)

(*MARIANA is leaning on the railing.*)
(*Change on the cyclorama. An unnatural light.*)

MARIANA: *The Conquest of the Atlantic* is an exciting book. I read it during the days I spent in the hospital in Akra. Almost three weeks under mosquito netting, listening to the drone of the fan. They didn't even have air conditioning. Fortunately the wound was a clean one. The bullet passed between my ribs without any complications. They told me I was lucky. So I can't complain. My trip to Africa was a story with a happy ending. Like a Hollywood movie. Domingo behaved beautifully. He stayed at my side the whole time. At night he would go back to the hotel. There weren't any beds in the hospital. When he would go, I would open the book and start reading. The noise of the fan would turn into the sound of the sea, and I would be off navigating with the Portuguese, searching for the southern route without knowing if it existed. I would be off hunting whales with the sailors of Ondarroa and Bermeo. And I would thrill as we marked the mysterious deviation of the magnetic needle as we passed into the great ocean like the captains of Christopher Columbus... But more than anything I enjoyed the story of the Abubakar expedition. Abubakar, emperor of Mali, intuitively sensed the existence of a continent across the waters long before the Spaniards ever reached it. The capital of his kingdom was Mopti, and every time that name appeared on the page, I would feel a strange emotion which brought me to the edge of tears, thinking about that fabled hero who dared to accept the challenge of the unknown and about whom nothing more was ever known. I liked to think that he finally reached his goal, and I would imagine him resting peacefully on some beach in America, all golden sand, refreshing breeze, and coconut trees, resting as I was resting on the white sheets of my bed.

(*Change on the cyclorama. Night.*)

(*LUCAS comes out of the cabin and walks to the railing.*)

MARIANA: Is he still sleeping?
LUCAS: Fast asleep. Don't worry, he'll be fine.

(*Pause.*)

MARIANA: When he's asleep, he's like another person. (*Pause.*) What has happened to us? My God, what has happened? (*Pause.*) I mean, this life is all we've got! (*Pause. LUCAS embraces her in silence. MARIANA returns the embrace.*) No. Let me go. (*LUCAS lowers his arms, but she continues the embrace.*) Let me go.

(*MARIANA moves away. The two remain at the railing looking out to sea.*)

(*Long pause.*)

MARIANA: Those lights?
LUCAS: Fishing boats. We're getting close to the coast. We'll be in Akra by dawn. (*Pause.*) I'm going to get my things.
MARIANA: Wait... (*LUCAS looks at her.*) I have to give you back your book.
LUCAS: Have you read it yet?
MARIANA: No... I started it, but I got to thinking about other things...
LUCAS: You can keep it.
MARIANA: No, no, I'll give it back to you.
LUCAS: Whatever you want.

(*Pause.*)

MARIANA: This is crazy.

(*Pause.*)

LUCAS: Why don't you come with me?
MARIANA: Well, you haven't asked me.
LUCAS: I haven't asked you?
MARIANA: Are you asking me?

LUCAS: Do I have to get down on my knees?
MARIANA: I don't even have a visa...
LUCAS: That's not a problem.
MARIANA: It's not?
LUCAS: No.

(*Pause.*)

MARIANA: But I don't know how to do anything.
LUCAS: Don't you want to learn?
MARIANA: In the hospital, what...? What kind of sicknesses do they treat?
LUCAS: We have everything. The most common, malaria. The most spectacular, leprosy.
MARIANA: Leprosy?
LUCAS: Does that scare you?
MARIANA: No. Really, no. Should it?
LUCAS: There hasn't been a single case of contagion. It's not like the movies... And you don't have to work in the hospital. We have a school at the Mission. And we're starting up a farmers' cooperative.
MARIANA: And, what will the priests say if they see me showing up with you?
LUCAS: We'll have to ask them. But another hand is always welcome.

(*LUCAS draws her toward him.*)

MARIANA: Yes, another hand is always welcome. (*MARIANA takes LUCAS's hand and looks at it.*) I have two hands, and I would need six.

(*They embrace in silence. They kiss passionately.*)

(*DOMINGO appears at the door of the cabin.*)

DOMINGO: I knew it. I knew it!

(*LUCAS and MARIANA separate.*)

(*DOMINGO raises his arm. He has the pistol in his hand.*)

DOMINGO: I ought to shoot you.
MARIANA: Why don't you?

DOMINGO: Because the pistol is unloaded.

(*MARIANA crosses toward DOMINGO.*)

MARIANA: Will you stop all this foolishness?

(*DOMINGO takes aim as if to fire.*)

DOMINGO: Pow!

(*A real shot goes off. MARIANA falls to the deck wounded.*)

(*Blackout.*)

(*On deck, MARIANA lying on a stretcher with intravenous hookup.*)

(*An ambulance siren is heard.*)

MARIANA (*Hurting from her wound*): Domingo!

(*DOMINGO appears loaded down with suitcases. He is carrying a bag of golf clubs on his back. He leaves everything on the deck and goes over to the stretcher.*)

DOMINGO: Easy. I'm here. Don't try to move.
MARIANA: What's that noise?
DOMINGO: The ambulance. Everything is taken care of. Don't be afraid. The doctor says you have an entrance and exit wound. They probably won't even have to operate. (*Pause.*) Mariana, I didn't mean to... I thought the pistol was unloaded...I swear I saw Lucas take the bullets out...., but the idiot must have left one in the chamber... You know I would never want to shoot...
MARIANA: Are we in Akra?
DOMINGO: Yes, in Akra. We got in this morning. They had us filling out papers all night...
MARIANA: And Lucas?
DOMINGO: He gave me this, for you.

(*DOMINGO gives her the Tuareg necklace.*)

DOMINGO: I helped him take down his baggage. You should have seen them unloading the Land-Rover off with a crane. The whole dock was full of natives watching it.

(*Pause.*)

MARIANA: What's going to happen now?
DOMINGO: Nothing. We said we were cleaning the gun, and released the safety. Plain accident... Unless you want to say otherwise.
MARIANA: I mean about us.

(*Pause.*)

DOMINGO: What do you say to starting over again?

(*Pause.*)

MARIANA: I wish I could have told him goodbye.
DOMINGO: You were sleeping like a baby. They gave you a sedative. Does it hurt? (*Pause.*) He did say goodbye to you. He gave you a kiss on the cheek.
MARIANA: Which side?
DOMINGO: I don't know. He told me. I left the two of you alone.

(*Pause.*)

MARIANA: Thanks.
DOMINGO: I think... you made quite an impression on him.
MARIANA: Maybe someday we could go visit him.
DOMINGO: Maybe. (*Pause.*) You know how many miles there are between Guinea and Mopti? The same as between Madrid and Moscow. (*Pause.*) How many times in your life have you been to Moscow?

(*DOMINGO takes her hand.*)

(*The light slowly fades out.*)

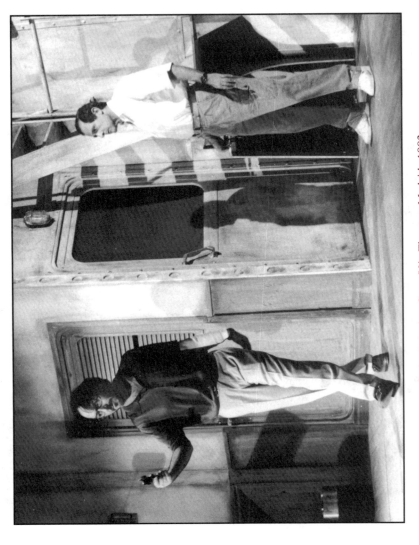

Travesía. Príncipe Gran Vía Theater, Madrid, 1993.
Directed by Fermín Cabal. Santiago Ramos and Emilio Gutiérrez Caba. Photo: Chicho.

CRITICAL REACTION TO CABAL'S WORK

"Rarely have I had occasion to find myself with a text which caught me up so much from the first reading. In the scenes of *Passage* I felt like the characters' traveling companion and, with them, at the rail of some merchant ship cutting its way through a sea of memories and expectations, of frustrations and hopes. I was given over to glimpsing, in the water's reflection, the hint of unexplored worlds, which, at any moment, we might embark upon."

Ernesto Caballero
Espiral edition of *Travesía*

"...the most representative work of Spanish theater of the decade."

Enrique Centeno
Diario 16

"Fermín Cabal leaves aside the author's ways of seeing characters as explained by Valle-Inclán -- from one's knees, standing beside, or from above -- he sits down with them and lets them talk about the hurt and the laughter of the human condition, about this miserable life of trying to get ahead in a world which only has one clear rule: if you lower your guard for a second, the other guy will K.O. you."

J. L. Alonso de Santos
Playwright

"Cabal's realism is everything that dramatic realism, understood up till now, is not."

Angel Ruggiero
Director

ABOUT THE TRANSLATOR

Rick Hite is Professor of Theater/Communications at Virginia Wesleyan College. While his teaching is principally in theater (acting and directing) and theater literature, he holds degrees in Spanish from Dartmouth College and The Johns Hopkins University and was Fulbright Lecturer in Spain in 1974/75. Among his translations are Alejandro Casona's *Siren Cast Ashore*, Alfonso Vallejo's *Train to Kiu* (*El cero transparente*) (ESTRENO, Contemporary Spanish Plays, 9), *Weekend*, and *Subterraneans* (*Gaviotas subterráneas*), Paloma Pedrero's *Bright Star* (*Una estrella*), and Fermín Cabal's *Get Thee Behind Me!* (*¡Vade retro!*) and *Castles in the Air* (*Castillos en el aire*). In 1996 his translation of *Dark Habits* (*Entre tinieblas*) by Fermín Cabal and Pedro Almodóvar was staged by the IATI at New York's American Theatre of Actors. It was directed by Angel Gil Orrios.

TRANSLATOR'S ACKNOWLEDGMENTS

I acknowledge a long-standing debt of gratitude to Martha Halsey, infinitely patient and efficacious editor of this series, and to Phyllis Zatlin for her invaluable advice in the preparation of this translation. I wish also to thank Professor Robert Russell of Dartmouth College for his continued encouragement, Virginia Wesleyan College for granting me sabbatical leave to undertake my translation projects, the Virginia Foundation for Independent Colleges for assisting me through the generous award of a Mednick Fellowship, and Theater Wagon of Virginia for providing a theatrical testing ground for this script.

ESTRENO: CONTEMPORARY SPANISH PLAYS SERIES

General Editor: Martha T. Halsey

No. 1   Jaime Salom: *Bonfire at Dawn (Una hoguera al amanecer)*
Translated by Phyllis Zatlin. 1992.   ISBN: 0-9631212-0-0

No. 2   José López Rubio: *In August We Play the Pyrenees (Celos del aire)*
Translated by Marion P. Holt. 1992.   ISBN: 0-9631212-1-9

No. 3   Ramón del Valle-Inclán: *Savage Acts: Four Plays (Ligazón, La rosa de papel, La cabeza del Bautista, Sacrilegio)*   Translated by Robert Lima. 1993.   ISBN: 0-9631212-2-7

No. 4   Antonio Gala: *The Bells of Orleans (Los buenos días perdidos)*
Translated by Edward Borsoi. 1993.   ISBN: 0-9631212-3-5

No. 5   Antonio Buero-Vallejo: *The Music Window (Música cercana)*
Translated by Marion P. Holt. 1994.   ISBN: 0-9631212-4-3

No. 6   Paloma Pedrero: *Parting Gestures: Three by Pedrero (El color de agosto, La noche dividida, Resguardo personal)*   Translated by Phyllis Zatlin. 1994.   ISBN: 0-9631212-5-1

No. 7   Ana Diosdado: *Yours for the Asking (Usted también podrá disfrutar de ella)*
Translated by Patricia W. O'Connor. 1995.   ISBN: 0-9631212-6-X

No. 8   Manuel Martínez Mediero: *A Love Too Beautiful (Juana del amor hermoso)*
Translated by Hazel Cazorla. 1995.   ISBN: 0-9631212-7-8

No. 9   Alfonso Vallejo: *Train to Kiu (El cero transparente)*
        Translated by H. Rick Hite. 1996.   ISBN: 0-9631212-8-6

No. 10 Alfonso Sastre: *The Tale of the Abandoned Doll   The Only Child of William Tell.* *(Historia de una muñeca abandonada. El único hijo de William Tell).*
        Translated by Carys Evans-Corrales. 1996.   ISBN: 1-888463-00-7

No. 11 Lauro Olmo and Pilar Encisco: *General Assembly.   The Lions.* *(Asamblea general.   Los leones)*
        Translated by Carys Evans-Corrales. 1997.   ISBN: 1-888463-01-5

A continuing series representing Spanish plays of several generations and varying theatrical approaches, selected for their potential interest to American audiences. Published every 6-9 months.

- -

ORDER FORM

Individual play/s. Prepaid. $6.00 including postage. List titles and quantities below:

Name and address:

Mail to: ESTRENO
          350 N. Burrowes Bldg.
          University Park, PA 16802 USA

Telephone: 814/865-1122
FAX: 814/863-7944

ESTRENO: OFERTA ESPECIAL

1	Ejemplar ....$13.00 ejemplar	Más de 10 ejemplares ....$ 7.00 ejemplar
2-5	Ejemplares ....$10.00 ejemplar	Colección completa.............$ 6.00 ejemplar
6-10	Ejemplares ....$8.00 ejemplar	

Vol. 1, * No. 1 (1975) Jerónimo López Mozo: **Guernica.**

Vol. 1, * No. 2 (1975) Romeo de Esteo: **Paraphernalia de la olla podrida, la misericordia y la mucha compasión.**

Vol. 1, * No. 3 (1975) Martínez Ballesteros: **Los placeres de la egregia dama.**

Vol. 2, No. 1 (1976) Arrabal: **El arquitecto y el emperador de Asiria.**

Vol. 2, No. 2 (1976) Lauro Olmo: **José García.**

Vol. 3, No. 1 (1977) Martín Recuerda: **La llanura.**

Vol. 3, No. 2 (1977) Ricardo Morales: **La imagen.**

Vol. 4, No. 1 (1978) Buero Vallejo: **La detonación.**

Vol. 4, No. 2 (1978) José López Rubio: **El último hilo.**

Vol. 5, No. 1 (1979) **"Buero Vallejo a través de los años"**

Vol. 5, No. 2 (1979) Jordi Teixidor: **La jungla sentimental.**

Vol. 6, No. 1 (1980) **Encuesta sobre el teatro madrileño de los años 70.**

Vol. 6, No. 2 (1980) Manuel Martínez Mediero: **Las hermanas de Búfalo Bill.**

Vol. 7, No. 1 (1981) García Alvarez y Pedro Muñoz Seca: **La casa de los crímenes.**

Vol. 7, No. 2 (1981) Pedro Salinas: **Los santos.**

Vol. 8, * No. 1 (1982) Luis Riaza: **Antígona...Cerda.**

Vol. 8, No. 2 (1982) Jaime Salom: **La gran aventura.**

Vol. 9, No. 1 (1983) Alfonso Sastre: **El hijo único de Guillermo Tell.**

Vol. 9, No. 2 (1983) Jorge Díaz: **Educación y un ombligo para dos.**

Vol. 10, No. 1 (1984) Víctor Ruiz Iriarte: **Juanita va a Río de Janeiro.**

Vol. 10, No. 2 (1984) Lidia Falcón: **No moleste, calle y pague.**
                                 Carmen Resino: **Ultimar detalles.**
Vol. 11, No. 1 (1985) Antonio Gala: **El veredicto.**
Vol. 11, No. 2 (1985) José Luis Alonso de Santos: **Del laberinto al 30.**
Vol. 12, No. 1 (1986) María Aurelia Capmany: **Tú y el hipócrita.**
Vol. 12, No. 2 (1986) Antonio Martínez Ballesteros: **Los comediantes.**
Vol. 13, No. 1 (1987) **Encuesta sobre el teatro de Valle-Inclán**
Vol. 13, No. 2 (1987) **Artículos sobre Buero, teatro postfranquista.**
Vol. 14, No. 1 (1988) Domingo Miras: **El doctor Torralba.**
Vol. 14, No. 2 (1988) **"Modern Spanish Drama on the Professional English-Speaking Stage"** (Número monográfico).
Vol. 15, No. 1 (1989) **Entrevista con Sastre, artículos sobre Carmen Resino, Lourdes Ortiz, Salom y Valle-Inclán**
Vol. 15, No. 2 (1989) Francisco Nieva: **Te quiero, zorra.**
Vol. 16, No. 1 (1990) **La mujer: autora y personaje.** (Número monográfico)
Vol. 16, No. 2 (1990) **Teatro español en Inglaterra, EEUU y Francia.**
Vol. 17, No. 1 (1991) Antonio Onetti: **La puñalá.**
Vol. 17, No. 2 (1991) Carlos Muñiz: **El caballo del caballero.**
Vol. 18, No. 1 (1992) **Teatro español e hispanoamericano.**
Vol. 18, No. 2 (1992) Antonio Gala: **Cristóbal Colón.**
Vol. 19, No. 1 (1993) Eduardo Quiles: **Una Ofelia sin Hamlet.**
Vol. 19, No. 2 (1993) Eduardo Galán Font: **La posada del arenal.**
Vol. 20, No. 1 (1993) José M. Rodríguez Méndez: **Isabelita tiene ángel.**
Vol. 20, No. 2 (1994) Concha Romero: **Allá él**
Vol. 21, No. 1 (1995) Jorge Díaz: **Historia de nadie**
Vol. 21, No. 2 (1995) Buero Vallejo: **Las trampas del azar**
Vol. 22, No. 1 (1996) Lauro Olmo: **El perchero**
Vol. 22, No. 2 (1996) Jaime Salom: **Una noche con Clark Gable**

* **Agotados.** Hay fotocopias disponibles a la venta

ESTRENO:
CUADERNOS DEL TEATRO
ESPAÑOL CONTEMPORANEO

Published at Penn State University
Martha Halsey, Ed.
Phyllis Zatlin, Assoc. Ed.

A journal featuring play texts of previously unpublished
works from contemporary Spain, interviews withplaywrights,
directors, and critics, and extensive critical studies in both
Spanish and English.

Plays published have included texts by Buero-Vallejo,
Sastre, Arrabal, Gala, Nieva, Salom, Martín Recuerda, Olmo,
Martínez Mediero, F. Cabal, P. Pedrero and Onetti. The
journal carries numerous photographs of recent play
performances in Spain and elsewhere, including
performances in translation.

Also featured are an annual bibliography, regular book
reviews, and critiques of the recent theater season, as well as
a round table in which readers from both the U. S. and Spain
share information and engage in lively debates.

ESTRENO also publishes a series of translations of
contemporary Spanish plays which may be subscribed to
separately.

Please mail to: ESTRENO
350 N. Burrowes Bldg.
University Park, PA 16802
USA.

Individual subscriptions are $15.00 and institutional
subscriptions, $26.00 for the calendar year.

Name   _____

Address   _____

            _____

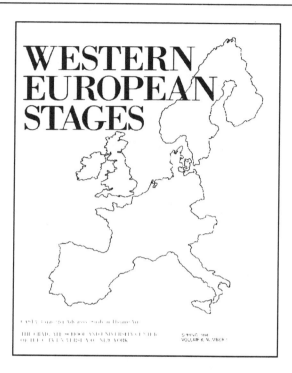

An indispensable resource in keeping abreast of the latest theatre developments in Western Europe. Issued three times a year – Spring, Winter and Fall – and edited by Marvin Carlson, each issue contains a wealth of information about recent European festivals and productions, including reviews, interviews, and reports. The 1996 Special Issue is devoted to contemporary women directors. Winter issues focus on the theatre in individual countries or on special themes. News of forthcoming events: the latest in changes in artistic directorships, new plays and playwrights, outstanding performances, and directorial interpretations. – $15 per annum ($19.00 foreign).

Please send me the following CASTA publication:

Western European Stages

___ @ $15.00 per year

(Foreign) ___ @ $19.00 per year

Total _____

Send order with enclosed check to:

CASTA, CUNY Graduate Center
33 West 42nd Street
New York, NY 10036